YOOMEE
(you-me)
and the Bully

Based on the book,
Yoomee and the Wonder Team — Ray Wilkins, Ph.D.

Written and Illustrated by
Patricia D. Wilkins and Ray G. Wilkins Jr. Ph.D. (Dr. "W")

Rule #1 – "All children have the absolute right to unrestricted love."
Rule #2 – "WE ARE ALL CHILDREN"

ISBN 978-0-615-38443-6
Published by Yoomee Adventures
An all volunteer 501(C)3 children's nonprofit organization
www.yoomee.org

Welcome, welcome, children of all ages.

May all sizes, all colors and

all shapes share these pages.

Before we begin, let's take in through our nose

A long deep breath from our head to our toes.

Now let it out slowly,

through your mouth slow and long

And flex your arms tightly and say,

"I am strong!"

Say "I am strong" until you believe it.

Now enjoy this story as you quietly sit.

Once upon a time in a place quite near here
Lived a little girl named Yoomee,
who was so very dear.
Her heart full of kindness, she was happy and glad.
But not long ago, Yoomee was sad.

You see, Yoomee was made of colors so bright.
Some children laughed and teased
when no teacher was in sight.
They could not see how beautiful she was.
They just whispered and pointed and created a buzz.

The biggest and meanest, Billy his name
Laughed louder than all, to him just a game.
When he made others cry, he was quite pleased.
He pushed and he shoved while he bullied and teased.
But the teasing hurt Yoomee, so deep down inside
That when no one was looking she sat down and cried.

On her way home from school, a rainbow appeared.

Its colors so glorious it almost brought tears.

And the flowers she saw of red, yellow and white

Brought joy to her eyes, a magnificent sight.

She thought, "If all the rainbow's colors were one

And the flowers one color, that wouldn't be fun."

So "Why?," she thought to herself so confused,
"Am I teased for my colors? There is no excuse.
If we all looked alike, how boring we'd be.
I'd look just like you and you'd look just like me.
There must be a way to help those who are teased."
Then she had an idea and Yoomee was pleased.

13

She gathered together those
who were teased and quite sad.
They all formed a team and
were glad that they had.
Their team would be helpful,
good deeds they would do.
They'd help those of all ages
and colors, it's true.
They'd learn to believe in
themselves and have fun.
They'd invite all the children
and include everyone.

They'd help clean up the parks,
the playgrounds and beaches.
They'd plant vegetable gardens
and trees full of peaches.
They'd collect food for the hungry
to show them they care.
They'd be good to all animals,
fish and birds everywhere.

They would help all the children,
they'd help far and wide.
When they helped others,
they felt happy inside.
They'd recycle the paper,
the cans and the glass.
They'd write a school play
and invite every class.
The play they'd perform
and the crowd would be pleased.
And on their new team
not one would be teased.
The plan was so simple
it almost seemed funny.
Their plan would be fun
and cost so little money.

Their play would tell all how they used to be sad
Because they let bullies make them feel bad.
But now they believed in themselves and were strong.
They all were so glad that Yoomee came along.
First they wrote the play's story with everyone in it.
Next, they had to rehearse so they could begin it.
They even asked Billy to be in the play
At first he just laughed, but then said, "Sure, okay!"
He said, "I'm so very sorry for the bullying I've done.
I'll be on your team and your play sounds like fun."

They worked very hard to get all things just right.

And before they knew it, it was opening night.

Their play had a story to tell, it was true

But it was also quite happy and fun for all, too.

Some sang and played songs while everyone clapped.

Some danced to the music, ballet, jazz and tap.

Some told silly jokes to make everyone laugh.

Some helped make the costumes
and were good at their craft.

Some painted the scenery, some turned on the lights.

Every one of them was part of this wonderful sight.

Even Billy, the bully was part of the show.

He recited a poem and how his words flowed.

"I used to be a bully, and Billy is my name.

But now I know that I was wrong

and I feel so ashamed.

It's much more fun to have

good friends, help others and be kind.

I'm thankful to be in this play

and I thank you for your time."

And with that Yoomee said, "Now, all of you, too
Can form your own teams, there is so much to do.
Believe in yourself and say "I am strong!"
And say it again and again all day long.
Your family, your friends, your teachers it's true
Can help you feel better and help you be you.
So when you feel sad or if you feel blue,
Remember to get some help for you, too.
Believe in yourself, don't let bullies rule.
Be strong in your heart and you will be cool."

The audience was happy,

the children were too.

They all were so proud

of the things they could do.

They were one together

as one Wonder Team.

Their play was a success

beyond all their dreams.

Thank you, thank you, thank you
and know that this is true.
You are strong and you are special.
Have fun and just be you.

YOOMEE ADVENTURES, an all volunteer 501(C)3 Children's Nonprofit Organization, would like to offer our sincere gratitude to our many friends, volunteers, contributors and supporters including, but not limited to:

Jamie Andrade... Kay Bunker... Eileen and Gary Brooks
Jarad, Jody and Nanci Busby... Fred Cox and family
Casey, Charley, Colby, Collin, Joanna, Justin, Kaitlin, Logan,
Mike and Priscilla Cagle and Bria
Ava, Brianna, Kendra, Mark, Melissa and Nancy Clemons
Gordon and Nancy Deans... Michelle Dionisio
Ms. Flemming's Kindergarten class, Cimarron Springs Elementary
Mary and Rick Gamble... Carolyn and Gerald Gelazela
Carlos and Gail Gonzales... Charlotte and Dale Heap
Genie and Joe Hilton... Harold Holloway
Michael, Patrick and Tom Johnson
Howard and Pauline Klemmer
Ms. Leti's 5th grade class, Cimarron Springs Elementary
Holly and Lou Marano... Jean and William McCurdy
Christy and Tim Merrell... Virginia and Tom Mont
Jeanna Michaels and Steve Katz... Pete Masterson
Dick and Pat Novotny
Dawn, Eric, Nicole Relyea and Chad Prunier
Ravenpheat Recording Studios... Barbara and Pete Rose
Carol, Keith, Lexi, Linda and Steve Ryan
Lois Schepel... Kelly and Mike Scott... Sally Sweeny
Len Truit and family
Janet and Stephanie Watson
Amanda, Carol, Jeremy, Logan, Pat, Ray and Vincent Wilkins
Jim and Sharon Wolcott
Angela and Ron Woodward

www.yoomee.org
webmaster Keith Ryan

Book assembled and coordinated by Pete Masterson,
Æonix Publishing Group, www.aeonix.com